T0359984

Live Joyfully

170 ways to lift your spirits

Patrick Lindsay

For
Lisa, Nathan, Kate, Sarah, Nic & Josh

This editon published by Affirm Press in 2020
28 Thistlethwaite Street, South Melbourne, VIC 3205
www.affirmpress.com.au
10 9 8 7 6 5 4 3 2 1

First published by Lime Tree Books in 2014
Suite 1401, 93 Pacific Highway, North Sydney, NSW 2060
www.patricklindsay.com.au

Title: Live Joyfully / Patrick Lindsay, author
ISBN: 9781925972221 (hardback)

 A catalogue record for this
book is available from the
National Library of Australia

Jacket design and illustration by Nicole Watts, Red Cloud Digital
Typeset in 10/12pt The Sans Ultra Light by Red Cloud Digital
Printed and bound in China by C&C Offset Printing

Change your default settings

Like digital devices, we start life on our default settings.
But that's operating at our most basic level.
To discover our true potential,
we must explore the outer limits of our settings.
We're works in progress,
the possibilities are endless.

'The great majority of men are bundles of beginnings.'
Ralph Waldo Emerson (1803-1882)

Gather mindful moments

Slow the daily rush.
Filter out past problems.
Take a child-like approach
And recognise the moment you're living.
Savour it as it happens,
rather than looking to the next one.

'Every morning we are born again. What we do today is what
matters most.'

Gautama Buddha (c563BC- 483BC)

Give kindness freely

Bestow kindness wherever you can.
Put no limits on it.
Seek no response.
Watch people's reactions.
Give it especially to those who seem the most difficult.
Often their responses are the most rewarding.

'The best portion of a good man's life is his little, nameless,
unremembered acts of kindness and of love.'
William Wordsworth (1770-1850)

Listen to your heart's whispers

Your heart is your true compass.
But only if you allow it to express itself freely,
and only if you listen to it.
Sometimes it's barely audible,
whispering its real feelings.
Listen for these, they are often the most valuable.

'Alas! There is no instinct like the heart.'

Lord Byron (1788-1824)

Meditate

Like defragging your computer,
meditation clears your mind.
It brings mindfulness and
encourages equilibrium.
It promotes inner feelings of calm and contentment.
It broadens your horizons.

'All things are ready if our mind be ready.'
William Shakespeare (1564-1616)

Value your time

The simple reality is there isn't time for everything.
We have no guarantees of how much time we have.
So we must respect it.
We must spend it wisely.
Not working every waking hour,
but living, loving and learning.

'What would be the use of immortality to a person who cannot use
well a half an hour.'

Ralph Waldo Emerson (1803-1882)

Control your body

Be aware of your posture.
Move with purpose.
Speak with authority.
Take your place proudly.
Lift your pace.
Your mood will follow.

'What you do speaks so loud that I cannot hear what you said.'
Ralph Waldo Emerson (1803-1882)

Fight complexity

Simple things are usually the most interesting.
And bigger isn't necessarily better.
Life is at its best when it's at its simplest.
Complexity can be suffocating.
Fight against it.
It's worth the crusade.

'Simplicity is the ultimate sophistication.'
Leonardo Da Vinci (1452-1519)

Create mind pictures

Envisage what you want to achieve.
Embed your goals in your subconscious.
They will act as a silent compass,
steering your decision-making,
and opening unseen doors,
on the path to realising them.

'Undoubtedly, we become what we envisage.'
Claude M. Bristol (1891-1951)

Find your style

Recognise and develop your own style.
Style always outlasts fashion.
Make sure your style is authentic.
Take advantage of your best attributes:
your personality, your presence, your voice.
Be comfortable with your style.

'Fashion is what you adopt when you don't know who you are.'
Quentin Crisp (1908-1999)

Have a mind-lift

Forget about face-lifts, look deeper than that.
Give yourself a mind-lift.
Work on improving your brainpower.
The options are many:
read voraciously, play mind games, do puzzles.
Change your perspective, look at other viewpoints.

'The mind is everything. What you think you become.'
Gautama Buddha (c563 BC – 483 BC)

Write your lifeline

Chart your achievements.
Give credit where it's due.
Place your life in its true perspective.
Take confidence from your successes.
Learn from your failures.
Aim for your goals.

'Not until we are lost do we begin to understand ourselves.'
Henry David Thoreau (1817-1862)

Die young, but live long

As we age we need regular mental software updates.
There may be some hardware glitches,
but updates can overcome most of them.
Turn newer with each day,
as you seek knowledge and new experiences.
Remember, if you don't use it (... *you lose it*)

'It takes a long time to become young.'

Pablo Picasso (1881-1973)

Develop focus

Above all, focus is the key to progress.
Without it, your skills and attributes are diluted.
With it, they are magnified and intensified.
Focus sets you apart from the also-rans.
It enables you to see through obstacles.
It clears the path to your goal.

'If you run after two hares, you will catch neither.'
Thomas Fuller (1608-1661)

Know your own secrets

Be brutally honest with yourself.
Only you know your innermost secrets.
They can be a positive or negative force,
depending on how you treat them.
Turn them into positives,
by taking responsibility for them.

'Everyone is a moon, and has a dark side which he never shows
to anybody.'
Mark Twain (Samuel Langhorne Clemens) (1835-1910)

Embrace your humanity

It's what sets you apart.
It's centred on your view of the world.
Make sure it's genuine, that it's yours.
Ensure you're not copying someone else's views.
When you're confident in your beliefs,
build on them, stay true to them.

'The privilege of a lifetime is to become who you truly are.'
Carl Jung (1875-1961)

Look inside

Ignore the external forces surrounding you.
The answers to our deepest questions lie inside us.
Here, you are in control.
You can choose your direction.
You can listen to your inner voice.
You make your choices.

'This above all: to thine own self be true.'
William Shakespeare (1564-1616) Hamlet (Act I, Scene III)

Withhold judgement

It's so easy to become a critic ...
after all, you need no qualifications.
Resist the temptation to join the naysayers.
Take the positive road.
Look for the light.
And, if something is wrong, consider how to fix it.

'Don't find fault. Find a remedy.'

Henry Ford (1863-1947)

Embrace your flaws

Perfection only exists in our dreams.
In real life it's unattainable and often unattractive.
Our imperfections set us apart as much as our
achievements.
Once we learn to accept them, we gain confidence ...
in our strengths, our resilience and our potential.
After all, if we reach perfection, there's only one
way to go.

Certain flaws are necessary for the whole. It would seem strange if old
friends lacked certain quirks.'
Johann Wolfgang von Goethe (1749-1832)

Count your blessings

The more we're thankful for what we've got,
the more we realise just how much we have.
Most of us are so far ahead of the game ...
family, loved ones, friends, lifestyle, nature ...
shortcomings in one are usually made up in others.
Look around in gratitude.

'All that we behold is full of blessings.'
William Wordsworth (1770-1850)

Greet the dawn

Every day welcomes you with opportunity.
It's a blank canvas awaiting your paintbrush.
With the dawn comes renewed hope.
Face it with relish.
Feel its warming embrace.
Let its growing energy recharge you.

'The sun has not caught me in bed for fifty years.'
Thomas Jefferson (1743-1826)

Downsize and declutter

Few activities are more empowering ...
than ruthlessly pruning accumulated possessions.
Few of us need the things or the space we acquire.
Retain the essential, and those with special meaning.
Make the rest justify their retention ...
or give them away.
You'll be invigorated beyond your expectations.

'It is preoccupation with possessions, more than anything else, that
prevents men from living freely and nobly.'
Bertrand Russell (1872-1970)

Come home to yourself

All the knowledge you acquire is available to others.
What sets you apart is how you use it.
Nobody has your unique combination of heart and
mind.
At the end of each day, be content to be you.
From that foundation you can build ...
a better you and a happier you.

'No one remains quite what he was when he recognizes himself.'
Thomas Mann (1875-1955)

Listen to what's not being said

Most of us hear people speaking.
What's more important is what they're not saying.
Look for the subtext.
Be aware of what has been left out.
Observe their revealing physical reactions.
Often the real message is in the omissions.

'The art of being wise is knowing what to overlook.'

William James (1842-1910)

Customs versus laws

What are presented as tried and tested laws,
may simply be long-held unchallenged customs.
Many don't stand the test of objective scrutiny.
They often serve as the basis for other assumptions.
When successfully demystified ...
they can open unexpected pathways.

'Forgive him, for he believes that the customs of his tribe are the laws of nature.'

George Bernard Shaw (1856-1950)

Learn your strengths

Just as others have to earn your respect,
so you have to earn self-respect.
One way is to honestly assess your strong points.
We all have them and they usually outweigh our
weaknesses.
Take the time to isolate your strengths.
Then use them wisely.

'He who knows others is learned. He who knows himself is wise.'
Lao-tzu (640BC-531BC)

Slow your eating

One of the best places to start savouring life ...
is during your meals.
Stop thinking of food as fuel ...
or worse, as comfort.
Eat slowly ... enjoy the taste, digest better,
lose stress ... and weight.

'There is more to life than increasing its speed.'
Mohandas Karamchand 'Mahatma' Gandhi (1869-1948)

Live now

Refuse to let time dictate your day.
Lose track of it.
Immerse yourself in whatever you're doing.
Surrender yourself to the activity.
Commit your full attention.
Notice the difference.

'The happiest of all lives is a busy solitude.'
Voltaire (François-Marie Arouet) (1694-1778)

Think for yourself

It sounds so obvious ... but look around and listen.
Many people's thoughts are not their own.
Many are recording machines on playback.
Consider your opinions before you air them.
Make sure you truly hold the viewpoint.
Then you can deliver it with passion.

'To find yourself, think for yourself.'

Socrates (469BC-399BC)

Seek experiences

It's not about the experiences themselves ...
but, rather, how you use them.
And not only are your experiences valuable.
You can learn much from others' experiences,
and especially from their mistakes.
It can save a lot of pain.

'Learning is experience. Everything else is just information.'
Albert Einstein (1879-1955)

Light up your life

We can live in shadow or in light.
We can choose to live in monochrome or technicolour.
Light comes from your heart.
It shines through the darkness
It acts as a beacon, drawing others to you.
Watch as they bask in it.

'When you possess light within, you see it externally.'
Anais Nin (1903-1977)

Evade the gatekeepers

Much that is valuable is obscured by life's gatekeepers.
These sentinels will try to deny you entry.
They see it as their duty to preserve the status quo.
To reach your goal you'll have to outwit them.
If you're determined enough, you'll do it.
Consider it the first step towards your target.

'Arriving at one goal is the starting point to another.'
John Dewey (1859-1952)

Stretch

Don't settle for comfortable.
Push yourself into the zone of uncertainty.
Find the challenges that will test you.
Find the satisfaction of achieving.
You'll answer many questions about yourself ...
questions that otherwise remain dormant.

'One may go a long way after one is tired.'

French proverb

Ignore the frames

Why be limited by the frames others put around you?
Don't allow your vision to be cropped.
Don't allow someone else to edit your dream.
Others don't know your limitless potential.
They are hampered by their preconceptions.
Only you can see the full picture.

'Is life not a hundred times too short for us to stifle ourselves?'
Friedrich Nietzsche (1844-1900)

Imagination rules

Look at the stories behind Apple or Google.
What imaginations envisaged them!
What perseverance brought them to fruition!
Only those giving their minds full reign achieve great things.
Your imagination is your greatest untapped asset, it holds new worlds to conquer.

'Imagination is the highest form of research.'
Albert Einstein (1879-1955)

Look for the pattern

Most situations develop to a pattern.
It may be camouflaged, or slow to reveal,
but it's usually there, and usually decipherable.
Understanding the patterns gives you power:
to anticipate the next steps,
or to break the pattern to find novel solutions.

'Habit rules the unreflecting herd.'

William Wordsworth (1770-1850)

Know your tribe

It doesn't matter what you call it:
a network; support group; family; clan; tribe.
We all need love, support, a haven.
In the worst of times, they are there.
Your tribe will forgive you.
They'll accept you and sustain you.

'Are we not two volumes of the same book?'
Marceline Desbordes-Valmore (1786-1859)

Find your faith

Don't follow blindly.
Look up, look around, observe consequences.
Filter according to your heart and common sense.
Seek articles of faith in which you'll find deep comfort.
These are your values.
Visit them often, explore them in depth.

'What matters is not the idea a man holds, but the depth at which he holds it.'

Ezra Pound (1885-1972)

Move to Trash

If you've proved that an idea or belief lacks merit,
jettison it without remorse.
Don't hold on to it from habit.
We never stand still.
Our ideas grow and change as we do.
Keep questioning and growing.

'The only man I know who behaves sensibly is my tailor; he takes my measurements anew each time he sees me. The rest go on with their old measurements and expect me to fit them.'
George Bernard Shaw (1856-1950)

Work in the crevices

The world never fits together perfectly.
There are always gaps.
Often they are windows of opportunity.
Shine a light into the crevices.
Work in there, somewhere between conformity and
chaos.
Great rewards reside there.

'Vision is the art of seeing things invisible.'
Jonathan Swift (1667-1745)

Get street-smart

There's study-smart and street-smart.
There's education and self-education.
The ideal is a combination of the two.
One without the other ultimately brings limitations.
But, if you have to choose,
err on the side of the street.

'A child educated only at school is an uneducated child.'
George Santayana (1863-1952)

Create

Our creativity is our endless source of energy.
It opens our mind's eye and fuels our adventures.
It travels with us and lifts our spirits.
It constantly duels with our better judgement.
Give your creative side a chance to thrive.
Encourage it every time it sparks.

'It's not what you look at that matters, it's what you see.'
Henry David Thoreau (1817-1862)

Who are you?

It's an intriguing question ...
but perhaps not the most important one.
The crucial one is: what might I become?
To know that, you need to know yourself.
And that is a gradual process,
because we are ever changing.

'When I let go of what I am, I become what I might be.'
Lao-Tzu (604BC-531BC)

Mind the media

Our formative media bears little resemblance
to our children's.
Once it was radio, TV, music, film, papers,
magazine, comics.
Now it's the internet, social media, Apps, games, etc.
Messages used to travel vertically.
Now they move horizontally ...
and parents are often the link that's cut out.

'The greatest thing about the internet is that you can write something
and completely make up the source.'
William Shakespeare (1564-1616)

Lose the pretence

We are only truly content as our authentic selves.
We wear our pretences for protection,
or because we fear we won't fit in.
They are temporary disguises.
And usually mask our better, real, selves.
Reveal the genuine you and embrace it.

'We are so accustomed to disguise ourselves to others that in the end
we become disguised to ourselves.'
François Duc de la Rochefoucauld (1613-1680)

Your eyes have it

Your digital camera has nothing on your eye.
Top cameras may have 20 megapixels.
Your retina has about 576 megapixels!
Buying a camera doesn't make you a great
photographer.
It only makes you a camera owner.
Use your eyes like a great photographer.

'The most pathetic person in the world is someone who has sight but no vision.'

Helen Keller (1880-1968)

Read the signs

Not the obvious signs, read the subliminal ones.
Poker players call them 'tells':
physical signals revealing true intentions,
intentions often contradicting the words uttered.
Develop your skills by constant observation.
It will pay great dividends.

'The power of accurate observation is commonly called cynicism by
those who have not got it.'

George Bernard Shaw (1856-1950)

Do a Google

Take the Google approach:
carefully examine your options,
prioritise them,
filter them by credibility and importance,
then chart your course.
Wisdom is using experience to choose.

'Life is the sum of all your choices.'

Albert Camus (1913-1960)

Travel first-hand

When making your decisions …
rely on primary sources,
or first-hand experience,
not on others' views.
That way, at least you make your own mistakes.
You don't blindly replicate those made by others.

'Trust yourself. You know more than you think you do.'
Dr Benjamin Spock (1903-1998)

Customise yourself

You haven't come off an assembly line.
You're a unique customised model.
Refuse to be defined by the labels they stick on you.
Insist on being the top of the line.
And that means adjusting to changing circumstances.
But never fear the upgrade.

'It's not the strongest of the species that survive, nor the most
intelligent. It is the one most responsive to change.'
Charles Darwin (1809-1882)

Lose the self-pity

If we stop being self-centred,
we change our viewpoint on everything.
We widen our horizons,
we start thinking about others instead of ourselves.
We break away from a strangling negativity.
We form a solid positive base.

'Self-pity is our worst enemy and if we yield to it, we can never do anything wise in the world.'

Helen Keller (1880-1968)

Prepare

How often have we seen chances go begging,
simply because we weren't ready to take advantage of
them?
Clearly we can't prepare for every eventuality,
but common sense will show us most of them.
Whenever you can, think ahead.
Prepare and be ahead of the game.

'He who is best prepared can best serve his moment of inspiration.'
Samuel Taylor Coleridge (1772-1834)

Don't do shy

Shyness simply isn't worth it.
It's based on a misapprehension:
that others find what we do, or how we
look, important.
Most of us are hit by shyness at some times
in our lives.
But do everything you can to overcome it.
It makes you miss out on too much.

'The shell must break before the bird can fly.'
Alfred Tennyson (1809-1892)

Shine

Don't just go through the motions.
Whatever you do, make it really worthwhile.
Stretch yourself, ignite your passions,
put your heart and soul into it.
The resulting energy will transform you.
And it will radiate to those around you.

'Some people are so much sunshine to the square inch.'
Walt Whitman (1819-1892)

Take time

Fight against the urge to rush.
Savour experiences,
explore their meanings,
learn from them.
Take the time to register your feelings.
Turn experience into wisdom.

'To live is to be slowly born.'

Antoine de Saint-Exupery (1900-1944)

Use your own typeface

Each of us has our own unique typeface ...
our handwriting.
It's almost as distinctive as our fingerprints.
Don't waste it, be proud of it, use it often.
Send handwritten letters and notes to friends and
loved ones.
Each one is a special gift.

'Beauty is God's handwriting ... a wayside sacrament.'
Ralph Waldo Emerson (1803-1882)

Make peace with the past

Come to terms with the past.
Learn from it.
Use it like a guidebook for the future.
But don't get bogged down in analysing it.
Visit it every so often to draw wisdom from it.
But, by no means, live there.

'Don't let yesterday use up too much of today.'

Cherokee proverb

Play with your pet

It's guaranteed to improve your mood.
It's scientifically proven!
Even playing with someone else's pet will work.
Take your dog for a walk ...
and spread the cheer to others.
Do it every day.

'Until one has loved an animal, a part of one's soul remains
unawakened.'

Anatole France (1844-1924)

Spend time with a close friend

It's better than any medicine,
and works like a human anti-depressant.
The familiarity, the shared memories,
will warm your heart and spark laughter.
Friends link us to our past,
and guide us into the future.

'Friendship is a sheltering tree.'

Samuel Taylor Coleridge (1772-1834)

Look ahead

Don't view life through the rear-view mirror,
Don't second-guess or recriminate.
Keep your gaze forward.
Look with anticipation,
with optimism,
untrammelled by the baggage of the past.

'There are far, far better things ahead than any we leave behind.'
C. S. Lewis (1898-1963)

Be a generalist

Our society glorifies the experts.
And certainly they have their place.
But let's give some credit to those with the wide view.
Let's support the all-rounder,
and appreciate their breadth of knowledge.
Let's strive for a balanced approach.

'There's nothing so stupid as the educated man if you get him off the thing he was educated in.'

Will Rogers (1879-1935)

Savour the scents

They are redolent of our lives' enduring memories.
Each brings back images snap-frozen in our minds.
The flowers, the trees, the ocean,
the perfumes, the after-shaves.
Welcome them back.
Revel in them.

'Pleasure is the flower that passes; remembrance, the lasting perfume.'
Stanislaus-Jean de Boufflers (1738-1815)

Sing your own song

Create your own melodies.
Write your own lyrics.
Draw them from your feelings and experiences.
Sing from the heart.
But make sure it's original ...
cover bands have little influence on the world.

'A bird does not sing because it has an answer. It sings because it has a song.'

Chinese proverb

Seek beginnings

Each time something ends, another thing starts.
So ignore the endings.
Focus on the new paths that open.
And treasure your first-time experiences.
They can't be repeated,
no matter how hard you try.

'A person often meets his destiny on the road he took to avoid it.'
Jean de la Fontaine (1621-1695)

Get more sleep

Make sure you allow your body to recover and repair.
Sleep deprivation has many negative impacts:
it dulls recall of the good times,
and enhances recall of the bad ones.
Sleep well, wake up positive,
And look forward to the day ahead.

'Fatigue is the best pillow.'

Benjamin Franklin (1706-1790)

Find fresh air

Break out of the boxes where you live and work.
Walk, sit, observe, suck in the air.
Feel the breeze move around you.
Watch the birds soar through it,
And the trees bend to it.
Even 20 minutes of fresh air will lift your mood.

'When you arise in the morning, think what a precious privilege it is to be alive – to breathe, to think, to enjoy, to love.'
Marcus Aurelius (AD121-180)

Impress yourself

In the end, there's only one person who can judge,
only one knows your true thoughts and feelings ...
you.
Forget about living up to others' expectations.
Create your own expectations,
and live up to them.

'At the centre of your being you have the answer; you know who you
are and you know what you want.'

Lao-Tzu (604BC-531BC)

Enjoy growing older

As we get older good things happen.
We become less judgmental.
We filter out negativity.
We emphasise the positive.
We value the days.
We appreciate life.

'There is an unspeakable dawn in happy old age.'
Victor Hugo (1802-1885)

Be a great memory

Enjoy every moment with your friends and family.
Don't hold back with your loved ones.
There are no guarantees on how long we have
together.
Make your time here count.
In the end, all we leave is love and memories.
Make sure you leave behind great memories.

'Memory ... is the diary that we all carry about with us.'
Oscar Wilde (1854-1900)

Cut the commute

If there's any way you can, lose the commute.
The long grinding wasted hours take their toll.
But if you're locked into a long journey to work,
do everything you can to enliven it.
Just don't get so enmeshed in technology,
that you can't appreciate the passing world.

'Only dead fish swim with the stream.'
Malcolm Muggeridge (1903-1990)

Don't magnify

Treat problems or triumphs with the respect
they deserve.
But no more.
Don't make them bigger than they are.
Discern the real from the perceived.
Keep them in perspective.
View with a healthy skepticism.

'Believe nothing, no matter where you read it, or who said it – even if
I have said it – unless it agrees with your own reason and your own
common sense.'

Gautama Buddha (c563BC-483BC)

Give others a break

Try not to be such a hard marker.
Allow for the vagaries of others ...
their unknown personal problems.
Give them the benefit of the doubt.
Make allowances for others ...
and yourself.

'It often happens that a man is more humanely related to a cat or dog
than to any human being.'

Henry David Thoreau (1817-1862)

One thing at a time

Multi-tasking is greatly overrated.
It can dissipate your efforts,
and cut your concentration span.
Do it when you must.
But when you can,
focus all your energies on the task at hand.

'The sun's rays do not burn until brought to a focus.'
Alexander Graham Bell (1847-1922)

Take the lead

When you know you're the right person,
don't wait for approval,
stand up and show the way.
Lead by example.
Encourage others.
Blaze the trail.

'Example is not the main thing in influencing others. It is the only thing.'
Albert Schweitzer (1875-1965)

Be brave

You don't have to be movie brave, or war brave.
It's often just acting because you know it's right,
even though you're scared.
When you follow your heart,
it's surprising how you find courage
you had no idea you possessed.

'Every man has his own courage, and is betrayed because he seeks in
himself the courage of other persons.'
Ralph Waldo Emerson (1803-1882)

Use a plate

Have a proper lunch.
Don't just stuff fuel into your mouth.
Take some time out.
Detach from the grind.
Dine.
You'll return to work renewed.

'We should look for someone to eat and drink with before looking for
something to eat and drink.'

Epicurus (341BC-270BC)

Live your truth

Mould your life around your beliefs,
not the other way around.
Lose your preconceptions,
and your truth will emerge.
Live your own truth,
not someone else's truth.

'There is no god higher than truth.'
Mohandas Karamchand 'Mahatma' Gandhi (1869-1948)

Reminisce

Reconnect with old friends.
Revisit old haunts.
Rediscover old photos and letters.
Bask in the warmth of the recollections.
Let the laughter flow.
Feel the spark of your spirit ignite.

'Things that were hard to bear are sweet in the memory.'
Lucius Annaeus Seneca (4BC-AD65)

Watch people

Observe those you meet.
Be curious.
Look past first the impressions.
Take note of the little details.
Learn from them.
That's where wisdom lies.

'Never trust to general impressions, my boy, but concentrate yourself upon details.'

Arthur Conan Doyle (1859-1930)

Look for the growth

It may not seem so at first,
but the darkest days often provide great opportunities.
Amongst the negativity and the turmoil,
there will be hidden moments.
Look for them.
They are chances for growth, for love and forgiveness.

'A man must make his opportunity, as oft as find it.'
Francis Bacon (1561-1626)

Exercise

It's one of the best ways to lift your spirits.
Walk, run, swim, play sport, go to the gym ...
get your blood pumping,
let your endorphins flow.
They'll promote positive thoughts
and change your day's trajectory.

'The first wealth is health.'

Ralph Waldo Emerson (1803-1882)

Use your tiredness

It's counter-intuitive but it works in practice:
try working when you're really weary.
If you're a morning person,
challenge problems at the end of your day.
Your normal preconceptions will be less rigid.
And often your brain will be more creative.

'Dwell not on your weariness, thy strength shall be according to the measure of thy desire.'

Arab proverb

Have a chat

Make a new connection,
or renew an old one ...
a friend, family member, workmate, stranger.
Learn about them, hear about their day.
Listen to their problems.
Put your problems into perspective.

'The most fruitful and natural exercise for our minds is, in my opinion,
conversation.'

Michel de Montaigne (1533-1592)

Rise with the sun

Synchronise with nature.
Wake with the sun, without a jarring alarm.
You create so many extra hours in your day ...
the golden hours, some of the most beautiful,
often stressless, hours in the day.
It's the best time for reflection or preparation.

'The sun is but a morning star.'

Henry David Thoreau (1817-1862)

Hold your dreams tight

What sets apart those who achieve their dreams,
and those who don't?
Persistence.
Refuse to give up on your dreams.
You may have to put them on hold sometimes.
But never abandon them.

'While he lives, he must think; while he thinks, he must dream.'
Isaac Asimov (1920-1992)

Ignore the inconsequential

Forget about annoying people,
unimportant things,
and small-minded opponents.
Adjust your mind higher.
Save your energies.
Focus on things that truly matter.

'Things that matter most must never be at the mercy of things which matter least.'

Johann Wolfgang von Goethe (1749-1832)

Be mindful

Mindfulness has been with us for millennia.
The ancients sought it through Buddhism.
Now the Western world is embracing it.
Even conservative medicine is adapting it.
Develop your own way of mindfulness.
Focus on the present without judgement.

'Be happy in the moment, that's enough. Each moment is all we need, not more.'

Anjeze Gonxhe Bojaxhiu 'Mother Teresa' (1910-1997)

Be thankful

We should be grateful for so many things.
Yet often we take them for granted.
Create a routine of thanking people.
Write to them personally, especially letters.
Let them know your true feelings.
It will bring deep satisfaction.

'Gratitude bestows reverence, changing forever how we experience
life and the world.'

John Milton (1608-1674)

Change your colours

Colours can affect our moods,
often subtly and unconsciously.
Each of us is affected differently.
Notice which colours bring you calmness,
and which stimulate.
Surround yourself with those that bring you peace.

'Colour is my day-long obsession, joy and torment.'
Claude Monet (1840-1926)

Inspire yourself

You can hardly expect to win others to your side,
if you haven't inspired yourself.
Sometimes inspiration comes unbidden.
Often you'll have to chase it down.
It's the spark that fires your imagination.
It's the dream that begets the goal.

'I dream my paintings and I paint my dream.'
Vincent van Gogh (1853-1890)

Don't hold back

Failing to express our real feelings,
can lead to profound regret.
We usually hold back out of fear,
or to avoid hurting others' feelings.
But judiciously speaking from the heart,
leads to deeper, more authentic connections.

'You have enemies? Good. That means you've stood up for something,
sometime in your life.'

Winston Churchill (1874-1965)

Be comfortable with yourself

Above all, accept your real self.
Recognise your weaknesses and work on them.
But also appreciate your strengths,
your differences,
your idiosyncracies.
Aim to be centred, not self-centred.

'Style is knowing who you are, what you want to say, and not giving
a damn.'

Gore Vidal (1925-2012)

Don't just survive, thrive

We write our own life stories.
We can stay in the wings,
and play an 'extra',
or we can write a leading role for ourselves.
We can leave our potential dormant,
or we can find greatness that lies within us.

'Go confidently in the direction of your dreams. Live the life you've
imagined.'

Henry David Thoreau (1817-1862)

Be the strength

Don't look for strength elsewhere ...
be it yourself!
Be the rock on which you, and others, rely.
Realise your potential by rising to the occasion.
Don't fear failure.
Just making the effort will win you great respect.

'Freedom lies in being bold.'

Robert Frost (1874-1963)

Look pressure in the eye

Try to take out the emotion.
View the situation dispassionately,
for what it is.
Look for ways to ease the pressure.
Set tasks, break them into manageable segments.
That way your vision will be clear.

'When it is dark enough, you can see the stars.'
Ralph Waldo Emerson (1803-1882)

Record your parents' lives

You'll honour them with your interest.
And provide a great legacy for your children.
You'll understand so much more about yourself.
You'll be amazed at the things you didn't know,
and surprised at their achievements.
Your respect for them will soar.

'When I was a boy of 14, my father was so ignorant I could hardly
stand to have the old man around. But when I got to be 21, I was
astonished at how much the old man had learned in seven years.'
Mark Twain (Samuel Langhorne Clemens) (1835-1910)

Go natural

You know it makes sense.
Seek balance with your diet:
Organic, unprocessed food, natural fibres, etc
Go easy on – or lose – the alcohol.
Look for nutrition suited to your age.
Make sure your body's fuel is Premium.

'Let thy food be thy medicine and medicine be thy food.'
Hippocrates (460BC-377BC)

Play on

Always foster your competitive spirit.
Keep playing games - physical and mental.
From walking and swimming to ball games,
to chess or cards or mind games.
Try to excel according to your skill or your age.
Set your own goals and go for them.

'Excitement is impossible where there is no contest.'
Henry Cabot Lodge (1902-1985)

Wear something you love

Your favourite clothes have a special aura.
They are impregnated with your memories.
They fold casually around your body.
They bring comfort.
They bring familiarity and security.
They make you feel yourself.

'Know, first, who you are; and then adorn yourself accordingly.'
Epictetus (55-135)

Explore your creativity

Don't accept your perceptions of your boundaries.
They're often formed by misguided experiences.
Ignore them.
Look at yourself afresh.
Ask: why not?
Explore fresh fields.

'It is our duty as men and women to proceed as though the limits of
our abilities do not exist.'

Pierre Teilhard de Chardin S.J. (1881-1955)

Treasure private time

Create your own cocoon,
a haven without interruptions or distractions.
Transport your mind and spirit there.
Do nothing.
Allow your mind to roam free.
Gain perspective.

'I will prepare and some day my chance will come.'
Abraham Lincoln (1809-1865)

Carry happiness

Share the warmth of your happiness.
Spread your smile.
It's your gift.
You worked for it, you own it.
Give it freely.
Others will reciprocate.

'Let us be grateful to the people who make us happy; they are the
charming gardeners who make our souls blossom.'
Marcel Proust (1871-1922)

Begin now

Our lives are not eternal.
Don't wait for some magic sign.
The sign is that you are here,
and your time starts now.
Work towards your dreams, your goals,
one step at a time.

'The future depends on what you do today.'
Mohandas Karamchand 'Mahatma' Gandhi (1869-1948)

Acquire a new skill

It doesn't matter what it is,
as long as you're passionate about it.
Open yourself to the exploration.
Push through the initial learning stage.
Absorb the knowledge with relish.
Enjoy the satisfaction of accomplishment.

'Whatever you are, be a good one.'

Abraham Lincoln (1809-1865)

Use your enthusiasm

It's the catalyst ...
to ignite your spirit,
put a skip in your step,
and a sparkle in your eye.
It's infectious.
It contains a special magic.

'There are only two ways to live your life. One is as though nothing is a
miracle. The other is as though everything is a miracle.'
Albert Einstein (1879-1955)

Embrace the wrinkles

Is there anything more soulless than the botox look?
Accept the wisdom lines,
and the grey or thinning hair.
Weave them in with your memories.
Take charge as you journey into the Third Age.
Go with pride and optimism.

'Experience is one thing you can't get for nothing.'
Oscar Wilde (1854-1900)

Keep your word

Respect flows to those whose word is sacrosanct.
Always honour your promises,
even if it brings disadvantage to you.
Think carefully before you commit your word.
Ensure you can deliver on it.
Once you give it, always keep it.

'It is not the oath that makes us believe the man, but the man the oath.'
Aeschylus (525BC-546BC)

Make something

Use your hands to make something tangible.
Do it with love and passion.
Paint, draw, build a table ...
whatever it is, put your heart into it.
And when it's finished,
give it away with love.

'The only gift is a portion of thyself.'
Ralph Waldo Emerson (1803-1882)

Evolve

Flow with the technological changes.
Don't slavishly follow every trend,
rather, stay flexible, and take a wide view.
Look at the broad trends and adapt to them.
Pick those that will allow you to maintain connections,
especially with your friends, families and colleagues.

'Anyone who stops learning is old, whether at twenty or eighty.'
Henry Ford (1863-1947)

Take a child to the zoo

Explore with them.
Feel their squealing delight,
as you open up new worlds of imagination and awe.
Be their guide,
as they ask the unanswerable questions.
Delight in their potential.

'Wonder is the beginning of reason.'

Greek proverb

Share love

Do it without conditions,
without boundaries.
Spread it around your family, your loved ones,
even your workmates.
Sow the seeds ...
that will flower down the years and leave a legacy.

'Who, being loved, is poor?'

Oscar Wilde (1854-1900)

Travel

Explore and learn about ...
your suburb, your town, your country, your world.
Keep your sense of adventure alive.
Broaden your horizons,
your knowledge,
your interests.

'One's destination is never a place, but a new way of seeing things.'
Henry Miller (1891-1980)

Take responsibility

Not just for your mistakes and failures,
but also for your successes,
and the problems that beset you.
They may not be your fault,
but it's your responsibility to react to them,
to find solutions, to change things.

'The price of greatness is responsibility.'
Winston Churchill (1874-1965)

Treasure your time

Our time is a non-renewable resource.
We each have a limited supply,
in our days, in our lives.
Treat it time with respect, prioritise its use.
Relish each minute.
Spend it wisely.

'Tomorrow is a new day; you shall begin it serenely and with too high
a spirit to be encumbered with your old nonsense.'
Ralph Waldo Emerson (1803-1882)

Find the fun

At home or at work, always try to find humour.
Even in the toughest, busiest moments,
lighten the work with enjoyment.
Keep things in perspective.
Keep the sparkle in your eyes.
A smile will brighten the day, and it's infectious.

'The most wasted of all days is one without laughter.'
e. e. cummings (1894-1962)

Look ahead

Don't waste precious energy on past failures.
Learn the lessons.
Apply them.
But move on from them.
Keep your focus on the future,
and the endless potential and possibilities it offers.

'And in today already walks tomorrow.'
Samuel Taylor Coleridge (1772-1834)

Read don't scan

Treat good writing with the respect it deserves.
It's fine dining for the mind,
not the fast-food of social media or the net.
Slow reading, like the slow-food movement,
brings out the richness of the craft,
and sets our imaginations alight.

'Show me a family of readers and I will show you the people who move the world.'

Napoleon Bonaparte (1769-1821)

Take a cold shower

No, not for the usual reason ...
but because cold water triggers our ancient dive reflex.
It slows down our metabolism to protect our body.
In turn, it reduces tension.
Negative thoughts often disappear with the shivers.
You're left with a lovely warm glow, and a new
mindset.

'Winter is on my head but eternal spring is in my heart.'
Victor Hugo (1802-1885)

Call a friend

When you're feeling down,
don't sit and stew on your own.
Talk it over with someone.
See or call a good friend or advisor.
Sharing the burden always makes it lighter.
And gives clues to the way ahead.

'The antidote for fifty enemies is one friend.'

Aristotle (384BC-322BC)

Eat seafood

Or walnuts ... whatever food is rich in omega-3.
These fatty acids have many benefits,
not least that people with diets rich in them,
are less likely to suffer from depression.
Like most things, these diets aren't a cure,
but they contribute to our overall wellbeing.

'One cannot think well, love well, sleep well, if one has not dined well.'
Virginia Woolf (1882-1941)

Re-create your strengths

Recall your most positive moments and thoughts.
Examine how you reached them.
Relive the feelings.
Remember them.
See how you can replicate the conditions,
and scale the heights again.

'Example is the school of mankind, and they will learn at no other.'
Edmund Burke (1729-1797)

Host a dinner

Bring together a balanced selection of friends,
in a warm convivial location,
preferably your home.
Allow the atmosphere to build naturally.
Help to interweave their interests.
Allow the magic to develop.

'Strange to see how a good dinner and feasting reconciles everybody.'
Samuel Pepys (1633-1703)

Defuse

When faced with a major problem,
talk it over with someone you trust.
Make sure you identify it accurately.
Try to contain your emotional reaction.
Stay in the present when responding to it.
Don't let it grow out of proportion.

'Never give up, for that is just the place and time that the tide will turn.'
Harriet Beecher Stowe (1811-1896)

Write your goals

It works like a road map.
It allows you to locate your position,
and later to check on your progress.
Writing down your goals prompts you to be specific.
And crystallises your thinking.
But you must act to achieve them.

'All know the way but few actually walk it.'

Bodhidarma (c500AD)

Daydream

It helps you to break out of your bubble.
It allows you to explore possibilities,
untrammelled by current problems.
It encourages you to time travel,
to enter others' minds,
and to look into the distance.

'He does not need opium. He has the gift of reverie.'
Anais Nin (1903-1977)

Play life's game

Life is a jigsaw puzzle.
You can only play with the pieces you're given.
But you can play it creatively.
The secret lies in seeing the connections.
And that comes from observation and experience.
With time the connections seem obvious.

'Commonsense is the realised sense of proportion.'
Mahatma Gandhi (1869-1948)

Surrender to music

Create your own music library.
Lose yourself in the rhythms.
Be transported by the stories and melodies.
Music starts where the words stop.
Let it wash over you.
Surrender to its mysteries.

'Music is the universal language of mankind.'
Henry Wadsworth Longfellow (1807-1882)

Set your own routine

We each work most effectively at different hours.
Some revel at night, some early morning.
Find when your mind sparks best.
If you can, break out of the 9-to-5 strictures.
Take control of your timetable.
Work your own hours.

'Time is what we want most, but what we use worst.'
William Penn (1644-1718)

Do what you love

And love what you do.
Lose yourself in your work.
Aim high.
Chances are you'll find yourself that way.
Trust what inspires you.
It will lift you to unexpected heights.

'Your work is to discover your work and then with all your heart to give yourself to it.'

Gautama Buddha (c563BC - 483BC)

Own your happiness

Don't hitch your happiness to others.
Don't link it to events outside your control.
See the distinction between events,
and your reaction to them.
You can only control the latter.
Your happiness depends on you.

'If you want to be happy, be.'

Leo Tolstoy (1828-1910)

Be a witness, not a judge

When you judge, your mind is closed.
You can't learn when you're judgmental.
Don't be a hard marker, of yourself or others.
Allow for life's vagaries.
Look for the positives ...
observe and learn.

'It is the property of fools to be always judging.'
Thomas Fuller (1608-1661)

Connect the dots

Observe the links,
see why people act and how things work.
Watch for the repetitions, see the patterns.
Wisdom is using experience ...
to understand developing situations,
and to solve problems.

'To a great mind, nothing is little.'

Arthur Conan Doyle (1859-1930)

Lose the distractions

It may seem counter-intuitive in the digital age,
but our world discourages connection.
And it militates against deep thinking.
Constant mental stimulation distracts.
Fight the distractions,
and promote your creativity.

'This perpetual hurry of business and company ruins me in soul if not in body.'

William Wilberforce (1759-1833)

Use limits positively

Just as Twitter forces us to be more succinct,
use your limitations positively.
Change your mindset.
View obstacles and borders as opportunities.
Reconstruct the possibilities.
Turn your thoughts into things.

'Some people grumble that roses have thorns; I am grateful that
thorns have roses.'

Alphonse Karr (1808-1890)

Find your heritage

It lies in the stories of your family and your tribe.
But look behind the stories for the truth.
Many were imperfect when handed down,
or were pure fabrications.
You may choose how heritage influences you,
but it will explain many things.

'Commonly men will only be brave as their fathers were brave, or timid.'
Henry David Thoreau (1817-1862)

Get a massage

Not only is massage a wonderful way to lose tension,
it boosts our mood.
It reduces our levels of cortisol, the stress hormone.
It promotes feelings of wellbeing.
It counteracts the impact of sitting all day.
It helps you sleep.

'There is more wisdom in your body than in your deepest philosophies.'
Friedrich Nietzsche (1844-1900)

Go to the source

Whether it's via Google or the library,
always seek primary sources.
Beware of second-hand views or conclusions,
especially those online, dressed as expert doctrine.
Keep asking questions.
And insist on finding the answers yourself.

'Research is the highest form of adoration.'
Pierre Teilhard de Chardin (1881-1955)

Use it

Notice how nature takes back anything not used?
It's the same with our bodies, our minds,
even our freedom or our democracy.
It's up to us to make sure we keep both active.
And the more we exercise our minds and bodies,
the more they reward us.

'The most difficult thing is the decision to act, the rest is merely tenacity.'

Amelia Earhart (1897-1937)

Smile your eyes

A simple smile has immense power.
It transforms your aura.
It warms a room.
It can even change a life.
Smiling your eyes drives tension from your face,
and invites a mirrored response.

'A smile cures the wounding of a frown.'
William Shakespeare (1564-1616)

Enjoy your own company

Solitude is your chance to refuel.
Take advantage of spare moments.
Allow your imagination to fly free.
Enjoy the rejuvenating quietness,
the chance to refine your soul,
and to reflect without pressure.

'The worst loneliness is not to be comfortable with yourself.'
Mark Twain (Samuel Langhorne Clemens) (1835-1910)

Open the windows

Feel the breeze,
and the fresh air as it brings renewal.
Watch the light fill the rooms.
Listen to the sounds of the street,
breathe in the new day,
open up to new ideas.

'A house without books is like a room without windows.'
Horace Mann (1796-1859)

Rearrange the furniture

It's a great way to change perspective,
to look anew at your home or office.
It will prompt you to clean unseen areas.
It will open new options.
It will galvanise your creative eye.
And lead to a refreshed environment.

'Those who cannot change their minds cannot change anything.'
George Bernard Shaw (1856-1950)

Blossom like a flower

Grow with slow purpose,
in harmony, and in your time.
Grow through your inner strength,
sustained by the power of your spirit.
And, at the right time,
bloom.

'Every flower is a soul blossoming in nature.'
Gerard de Nerval (1808-1855)

Cradle a baby

It brings an immediate connection like no other,
heart straight to heart,
as the miracle of life is personified.
The unique scent of infant innocence,
the aura of trusting helplessness,
all redolent of unlimited potential.

'Life is a flame that is always burning itself out, but it catches fire
again every time a child is born.'

George Bernard Shaw (1856-1950)

The best is yet to come

The rest of your life ...
should be the best of your life.
You have the power to make it so.
Look up and ahead:
remember, whatever stage you're at ...
it's not your final destination.

'There is no end. There is no beginning. There is only the passion of life.'
Federico Fellini (1920-1993)

Meet your hero

You may be setting yourself up for disappointment.
Your heroes may have feet of stone.
But maybe that's not really important.
It's what they mean to you, what they stand for,
and what they inspire in you,
that makes them important.

'As you get older is it is harder to have heroes, but it is sort of necessary.'
Ernest Hemingway (1899-1961)

Credit the effort

Change your focus.
Give credit to yourself, and others,
and especially your kids,
for the effort,
not just the successes.
It will inspire them to greater heights.

'When you cannot get a compliment in any other way pay yourself one.'
Mark Twain (Samuel Langhorne Clemens) (1835-1910)

Embrace your potential

We all have untapped potential.
It lies within us awaiting our call.
Its greatest enemy is often fear,
or lack of confidence.
The only thing preventing us reaching it ...
is us.

'If you hear a voice within you say "you cannot paint", then by all means paint, and that voice will be silenced.'
Vincent Van Gogh (1853 -1890)

Get in the zone

Sporting champions aim to play 'in the zone'.
There they transcend conscious thought,
to play instinctively at their optimal level.
We can do it by immersing ourselves in work we love,
which inspires us so much,
that we lose track of time.

'The most important weapon on earth is the human soul on fire.'
Ferdinand Foch (1851-1929)

Take a small step

Staging is the secret to so many things.
At first view many goals are enormous.
Some simply appear unachievable.
But divide them into smaller sections,
stages that can be easily envisaged,
and you'll transform the journey.

'Progress is not accomplished in one stage.'

Victor Hugo (18802-1885)

Pause on a roll

It's tempting to go hard on any task,
until you're exhausted.
But it's much smarter to take a break,
while you still have something in the tank.
That way, when you resume,
you can power on from where you left off.

'It does not matter how slowly you go as long as you do not stop.'
Confucius (551BC-479BC)

Join your head to your heart

Aim to align your values and your actions.
Happiness lies there.
Interweave your heart and your mind.
Consider it a work in progress.
Don't look for perfection.
Instead, concentrate on the effort.

'One ought to hold on to one's heart; for if one lets it go, one soon
loses control of the head too.'

Friedrich Nietzsche (1844-1900)

Find the trade-offs

Life is rarely definitive.
Usually it's a series of compromises,
between desires and possibilities,
hopes and realities,
achievements and fulfillment.
Seek fulfillment.

'Compromise is the best and cheapest lawyer.'
Robert Louis Stevenson (1850-1894)

Read every day

Fiction or non-fiction, book or tablet.
It's not about the package, it's about the ideas.
Great fiction will inspire, transport you,
open your mind and heart.
Great non-fiction will inform,
and broaden your world.

'I guess there are never enough books.'

John Steinbeck (1902-1968)

Tell stories

Especially tell your unique tales.
People will learn more about you.
You'll learn more about yourself.
Your stories validate your life choices.
They explain your history.
They bring you, and your listeners, closer.

'If history were taught in the form of stories, it would never be forgotten.'

Rudyard Kipling (1865-1936)

Chat to strangers

Sure, pick your time and the person,
but trust your instinct.
Connect with your eyes, open your heart.
It's amazing what you'll learn.
You'll spread warmth,
and confirm humanity.

'There are no strangers here; only friends you haven't met yet.'
William Butler Yeats (1865-1939)

Appreciate success

Especially the success of others.
It's easy to feel jealous,
and begrudge them their achievements.
But most are being rewarded for their hard work.
Use it as an example.
Follow in their footsteps, and beyond.

'Life is too short to be little.'

Benjamin Disraeli (1804-1881)

Treasure your humanity

Don't take it for granted.
Value it in yourself and in others.
Fight to retain and foster it.
Alllow your real feelings to reign.
Let them steer you,
towards the beautiful things in life.

'We are healthy only to the extent that our ideas are humane.'
Kurt Vonnegut (1922-2007)

Speak the truth

It can require great courage.
And it's often the hard path,
especially when it shows you in a bad light,
or as the one against the crowd.
But have it as your aim,
or you'll find yourself replaying lost opportunities.

'Be truthful, gentle, and fearless.'
Mohandas Karamchand 'Mahatma' Gandhi (1869-1948)

Ignore the shortcut

It's so tempting to cut corners.
But often it ends up being destructive.
Take the time.
Do it right.
Do the hard yards.
Reap the full reward.

'Act as if what you do makes a difference. It does.'
William James (1842-1910)

Ask for help

Very few things are done better alone.
And team achievements are invariably sweeter.
Asking for help reminds people of their value.
It's a compliment, a sign of respect.
But do it to their timetable.
And give them their credit.

'It is one of the most beautiful compensations of this life that no man
can sincerely try to help another without helping himself.'
Ralph Waldo Emerson (1803-1882)

Try differently

If it's not working, simple repetition won't solve it.
Pause, reassess, look at the problem anew.
Before trying again, or trying harder,
look from a different angle.
Then try it smarter,
and do it differently.

'The only way to avoid making mistakes is to have no new ideas.'
Albert Einstein (1879-1955)

Give yourself

Whether it's your time, your heart or your money.
It's a scientifically-proven fact,
showing kindness to others,
helping them in almost any way,
brings an immediate increase ...
in your wellbeing.

'For it is in giving that we receive.'

Francis of Assisi (1181-1226)

Plan a journey

The strange thing is ...
you don't actually have to take the trip.
Just start making plans for it.
The anticipation of planning your journey,
boosts your happiness levels,
for many weeks.

'The real voyage of discovery consists not in seeking new landscapes,
but in having new eyes.'

Marcel Proust (1871-1922)

Value your down time

Especially as you get older,
relaxation time is far more valuable than money.
It returns so many more benefits,
to your family,
your health,
your happiness.

'Take rest; a field that has rested gives a bountiful crop.'
Ovid (43BC-AD17)

You're not your work

Your work doesn't measure your worth.
It shouldn't define you,
to others, or to yourself.
Your work won't last forever.
Don't let it dominate your views,
or your lifestyle.

'What the superior man seeks is in himself; what the small man seeks
is in others.'

Confucius (551BC-479BC)

Break out of busy

We're busy most of the time.
But don't let it become an excuse to procrastinate.
Successful busy people find the time,
to deal with their work,
to be with their families, and loved ones,
and to care for their health.

'It's not enough to be busy, so are the ants. The question is, what are we busy about.'

Henry David Thoreau (1817-1862)

Review the facts

When emotions run high,
and things threaten to get out of hand,
mentally step back,
and take yourself out of the picture.
Revert to the facts.
Argue and choose purely on those facts.

'Evolution is a light that illuminates all facts, a curve that all lines
must follow.'

Pierre Tielhard de Chardin (1881-1955)

Retain your power

No matter how great the pressure,
or how confused the situation,
hold tight to your personal power of choice.
You always have the final say,
to make your own choices,
according to your own beliefs.

'Life is the sum of all your choices.'

Albert Camus (1913-1960)

Focus on others

In the end, it's not about you.
In fact, there's you ...
and the rest of the world is others.
The more you turn your attention away from yourself,
the more you open your heart,
the more your mind will follow.

'True humility is not thinking less of yourself, it is thinking of
yourself less.'

C. S. Lewis (1898-1963)